VENEZUELAN

VERNACULAR

Text by
Federico Vegas

Photographs by
Federico Vegas
Ramón Paolini
Martín Vegas

Published by
Princeton
Architectural
Press

Produced by
Mondo
Graphico

Princeton Architectural Press
40 Witherspoon Street
Princeton, New Jersey 08540

© 1985 by Federico Vegas
and Princeton Architectural Press
All rights reserved
Published 1985
Printed in Italy
89 88 87 86 85 5 4 3 2 1
ISBN 0-910413-05-3

Editor: Judith McClain-Twombly
Designer: Kevin C. Lippert
Repro by CLG Verona
Printed in Italy by
Offset Print Veneta Verona

Our endeavor to gather aspects of Venezuela's architectural vocabulary was conceived initially as a set of pictures, a series of urban and architectural solutions, presented as a silent catalogue. The image alone was to represent our subject because the word, we reasoned, had little to offer.

The literature that accompanies these pictures will not fall upon the protagonists of this book, the people that built the towns, streets, windows, doors, houses, and churches presented here. We know in advance that we cannot establish a real relationship with the vernacular. We may demonstrate its forms, but we cannot establish a direct dialogue with the process that generates these forms. The literature on vernacular architecture is a literature of opinion only, sometimes arrogant, always distant and unattached.

We must preface the following text with an acknowledgement of our limitation: the inability to reach beyond approximation, beyond statements that cannot be verified or settled. Perhaps a reason for this disadvantage is that we must use methods of expression and analysis that differ from those used by the vernacular to review itself and endure. The literature on vernacular architecture consistently reveals this problem of the distance between two cultural situations: that of the narrator and that of the subject.

Let us analyze a conspicuous example. In the time of Emperor Augustus, the Roman architect Vitruvius wrote what is considered the first treatise on architectural theory, *The Ten Books on Architecture.* In the second book he comments on "The Origin of the Dwelling House." After he describes the form and technique of the first roof, he states, "That houses originated as I have written above, we can see for ourselves from the buildings that are to this day constructed of like materials by foreign tribes: for instance, in Gaul, Spain, Portugal, and Aquitaine...." Vitruvius used what was current in other nations as proof and example of the primitive origins of the Roman house. Consequently he believed that what was then current in Rome would become the logical future for Spain, Gaul, Portugal, and Aquitaine; to a great extent his prediction was correct.

We will look at the material in this book through modifications of, and coincidences with, Vitruvius's statement. The buildings that follow are also "to this day constructed" and resemble their vernacular origins; but from this coincidence between our past and present, we intend to foresee our architectural future.

It may be argued that Vitruvius's statement is appropriate only in the context of primitive architecture; but I believe that in establishing a relationship between primitive forms and Roman architecture, the dominating culture — the vernacular — was implicit. But why? How can we define the vernacular? How does it differ from primitive or popular architecture?

What we can state easily about primitive architecture is the precision of its architectural vocabulary, the strength of the relation between its solutions and its particu-

lar problems. We accept that it grows within a single culture, circumscribed to its limits. Right or wrong, we tend to look harder at primitive architecture for internal clues rather than exterior influences, for ancestral customs rather than recent changes.

Popular architecture invites a different discourse: *popular* suggests something new and foreign that affects something established. Popularization implies that something, be it assimilated or imposed, is being interpreted, transformed, adjusted, or absorbed. Popular architecture, then, is dynamic, occurring between process and change.

The nature of vernacular architecture is more static than that of popular architecture. The term *vernacular* derives from the Latin word *verna,* meaning "a slave raised in the household of his master." Its etymology suggests the peculiarities of vernacular architecture: it is an architecture molded to the image of another. "The slave" modifies and interprets those forms with which "his master" confines and dominates him. Although both vernacular and popular presuppose an influence, they differ in the character and stage of that influence: the vernacular is a historical fact, that which has already taken place; the popular is an act in process, that which is *becoming* history.

The etymology of each term follows the history of Spanish-American architecture, which is the basis of our present popular and vernacular architecture. Popular also means, or used to mean,

"to populate," and to populate the American continent was Spain's goal. It can be said that through the town Spain popularized a doctrine and an economy; this task was so prodigious that within three centuries Spanish towns covered the continent from the extreme south up to the western states of the present United States. Each town was built in homage to the "house of the master," and began with a plaza, a church, and the symbols of the Crown.

The meanings of vernacular and popular are well represented and almost welded in the peculiar historical process that began with our cumbersome and violent incorporation into Western civilization through Spain. The following images are linked directly to this process and its consequences and transformations.

LANDSCAPE

A fter the fifteenth
century, Spanish captains
and missionaries began
arriving on our shores in
an enterprise of faith and war; they
represented an empire resolved to
populate and open roads in the
new continent — as far, as fast,
and as homogeneously as possible.
Since Spain knew nothing about
the continent, "possible" and
"impossible" were not parameters.
The men who initiated the
encounter between Europe and
America did not know how many
towns they would found nor the
length of the routes they would

travel; they confronted a territory and destiny undefined. Gradually one town became a point, two a line, and three, at last, a territory that could be called the Crown's own.

Early European settlements in America were built around the ship, the only major artifact brought from Europe. Columbus constructed the first European building in La Española on his initial voyage: he turned his own Santa María upside down in the sand to become a most ephemeral fortress. The first French pioneers in Florida also built an ephemeral fortress, but this fortress was transformed into a ship, by which they tried unsuccessfully to return to France.

In 1497 Queen Isabella of Spain gave Columbus a list of supplies that she granted him for his third voyage. There is little on this list about towns or architecture; she mentions two large tents and recommends that supplies be taken in an old ship, which could be dismantled and used in the construction of a town.

Everything about the continent itself was ignored: existing cultures, building materials, food, climate, rivers, and limits — the real meaning and extension of the "new."

It took some time before Spain ceased to search for the Ganges; in the meantime she was caught by a delirious desire to expand. Before they really knew the local geography, the Spaniards had founded and transformed hundreds of towns. Founding a town was simple: it took only thirty neighbors and a five-league radius of land.

Obviously the recipe of the ship had to be abandoned as a means of urbanization. What became its substitute? How were sites chosen in a foreign landscape, one that constantly invited fantasy and the obsessive search for riches? The settlers had two resources at hand. The first was the existing "urban plan" of pre-Columbian cultures. An existing town meant a nourishing landscape; a magnificent city like Cuzco or Tenochtitlan meant, of course, much more. In Venezuela,

however, the Spaniards came not upon big cities but small towns, which offered hundreds of years' experience with a particular landscape. The second resource was a European urban tradition that dated back centuries, an approach to urbanization based on the grid and the plaza. Throughout history the grid proved ideal for creating new towns. An example of its success had been the Roman Castrum, and for the sixteenth and seventeenth centuries it was to be the Spanish-American city.

During the Renaissance the idea of a new town based on a regular structure was developed as a practical and ideal urban solution. Vitruvius's *Ten Books on Architecture*, rediscovered in 1414 and popularized in many editions since 1486, played an important part in this process. The *Ten Books* in turn influenced the most complete and clear body of rules

concerning the Spanish-American city: the "Ordinances for Discovery and Population," dictated by King Phillip II in 1573. Although by this date Spain's urbanizing work in America was well under way, these ordinances guided and consolidated a process begun under other, previous influences.

Through the Middle Ages Spain kept the tradition of the grid and plaza as a solution for creating new towns. Isidore of Seville and Alphonse the Wise, among others, contributed to a theoretical body that served as a text for urbanization. Other examples included the remains of cities built in Spain by the Romans and the few towns built by Spanish kings during the wars of reconquest against the Arabs. This set of theories and traditions met in the American continent a new geography with extremes and situations hitherto unknown. To choose sites in jungles, coasts, plains, and mountains; through heat and cold, high and low; from that which was similar to Castille to that which varied from it: all represented the beginnings of adaptation to the New World. Selecting a site for the grid and plaza was one of the first acts of interpreting and understanding the continent.

Left: Agua Larga
Right: Paraguaná

Clockwise: Pueblo Nuevo • Piñango • San Luis de la Sierra • Laguna de Sinamaica

The range of circumstances that a centralist empire such as Spain had to control called for the repetitive and abstract character of the grid: abstraction in the face of uncertainty, cohesion in the face of diversity. What were ideal principles for the Renaissance became urgent and practical needs for Spain. For example, Alberti's idea that continuity between urban elements generates one element within another, beginning with the selection of region and platform, became for Spain a requisite for the creation of a homogeneous self-image in a new and ever-changing landscape. The empire needed a clear, concise vocabulary; the grid was an ideal "board" on which to build towns from a distance, with little communication and in a spectrum of sites.

Spain had to tame and make sacred the infinite, profane landscape of America to initiate her urbanizing plan. Once the site was chosen, a series of acts and rituals was performed to give the endeavor legal value: the townspeople made a public declaration, indicating that possession was taken in the king's name; with a sword they incised a tree (if a tree was unavailable, they planted a trunk in the ground with

its branches removed, or uprooted grass, or hurled stones through the air, or carved a cross somewhere); then everyone swore to defend the town. Any gesture that modified the landscape sufficed to indicate the birth of a village, which usually remained on the first site proposed; sometimes a town moved frequently, perhaps to the opposite bank of the river, upstream or downhill — like a portable town.

In other instances the "town" was merely a name attached to a schematic drawing that traveled in the saddlebag of the conquistador on his unending journey to the most hidden and lush American landscape, never to be founded at all.

In general, the vernacular town is thought of as an enigmatic entity built without preconceived form or compositional rules, generated casually in its site. Such is not the case with towns in which most of our vernacular architecture exists today. They evolved from the same will that endures in the most diverse geographical situations. Today we have the opportunity to observe a single urban idea in a hundred different settings, a variety that as a whole obeys the rules that to this day are legible and reproducible.

Pedregales

T O W N

We have discussed that the urban theories and practices applied to Spanish America derived not only from the Italian Renaissance, but also that, via the Spanish Middle Ages, the Roman urban effort influenced the fifteenth- and sixteenth-century urban practices of the Spanish Empire. One of the links in this chain was King Alphonse the Wise, and one of his many works is *The Book of Chess, Dice, and Tables.*

Overleaf: San Isidro de Ceuta
This page: Playa de Pedro González

The introduction to his treatise tells how these games served originally as models with which three wise men instructed a certain king of India on the fundamentals of "facts and things." The first wise man believed that the fundamentals were founded on reason, and thus he presented the king with the game of chess; the second wise man believed they were determined by chance, and he gave the king a pair of dice; the third wise man submitted what we now call the game of backgammon, for he believed that the fundamentals relied on prudence or good sense, the balance of chance and reason.

Alphonse the Wise may have had ulterior motives when he presented this treatise to his subjects. In 1248 Alphonse's father, Ferdinand the Saint, had recaptured Seville from Moor domination; following Ferdinand's death, it was Alphonse's lot to reign during complex times over a heterogeneous realm, in which Christian, Arab, and Hebrew cultures coexisted. The King had to teach his subjects the principles of order and hierarchy: chess was an effective medium to explain and popularize the mechanisms of a kingdom, its components, and how they moved and interacted according to determined functions in a regular, homogeneous, precise, and reproducible space.

Despite his important intellectual output, Alphonse the Wise had a tragic finale. He sought the title of Holy Roman Emperor and almost captured it; but his "campaign" expenses led his kingdom to bankruptcy. His life ended in Seville, besieged by the troops of his son, Sancho the Angry.

There are a few coincidences between chess and the Spanish-American city. One is the repetitive and reproducible character that they share, which is based on easily transmitted principles that in time generate infinite variations and combinations. Another coincidence is their underlying principle, used as a propaganda instrument in Spanish-American urbanism: the idea of order and regularity. A third connection is the universality of each: like the chess board, the scope and origin of the grid and plaza date to imprecise, faraway times.

During the following three centuries Spain regained control of the rest of her territory, extended her domain to the greater part of the American continent, and at last had as king a Holy Roman Emperor, Charles I of Spain. I will end this story of the *Book of Games* with Charles's son, Phillip II, who built the Escorial monastery — a combination of palace, tomb, and city — and who brought to the Escorial library Alphonse's *Book of Games*, then as now wrapped in leather with drawings of square patterns, much like a chess board, the plan of the Escorial, and the grid of the Spanish-American city.

I have told such a distant, speculative story because it offers a series of provoking relationships within the awakening in medieval Spain of classic ideas about urbanization. The city grid was not modeled after the chess board; Alphonse the Wise knew by heart the Roman military manuals and through them about the Castrum. In many of his works he refers to the grid as an urban form; he even built a version of the grid at Tablada — one of the

El Morro de Puerto Santo

encampments from which he and his father laid siege to Seville in 1248.

Tablada was a provisional city of poles and tiles but organized as a perfect grid. More than two centuries after Tablada's founding, the Catholic rulers Ferdinand and Isabella used a similar plan while besieging Granada; again, the same plan was adopted for the first permanent settlement in America, the city of Santo Domingo.

Let us turn now to an example of how a town was founded in Spanish America. Pablo Vila recounts the origins of Nueva Barcelona, situated on the Caribbean coast of Venezuela, in his book *The Feat of Juan de Orpí.* After advancing five months through hostile territory, an expedition led by Juan de Orpí reached the banks of the Neverí River. Here the expedition found a suitable place for building a town and set up tents near the site. The camp soon settled, and rustic (but still temporary) log cabins replaced the tents, always close to, but not

yet on, the chosen site. Before the town was built they had to assure a continuous food supply. The expeditionaries, already turned into settlers, divided themselves into groups that farmed, fished, built corrals, and fought local Indians. A year of these preliminary arrangements passed before they built the definitive town. Vila tells the following story about Nueva Barcelona:

This specific town plan was to be in the shape of an elongated quadrangle, along the river, and the area to be urbanized was cut by right-angled, intersecting streets, from which resulted squared lots to be divided into four parcels, one per angle. At the center, on the bank of the Neverí, the median lot was reserved for communal use by all neighbors; it would become the city plaza, which would serve both as a pier and as the center of convergence for traffic and out-of-town roads. A street would border the bank of the Neverí, and the church and the town hall would face the plaza.

All those that remained would cast lots to distribute the land among themselves, and they began by moving their tents to their place. Some started by building a hut; after a while, it became evident that all should help each other {build the definitive house}.[1]

Still Nueva Barcelona needed a ceremonial act to make it official. The would-be city was but ninety people, a few markings on the ground, huts of sticks and straw beside a porch that served as a church; in all, somewhat smaller and weaker than Alphonse the Wise's Tablada encampment. On founding day a lot of people arrived, even from distant towns. For the occasion the settlers produced packsaddles, helmets, and wild flowers; present were a priest, an altar, guards, Indians, trumpets, and notaries; they held a mass, gun salutes, and the appointments of the mayor and councilmen; finally the city was founded. "City," we have to say,

San Juan de las Galdonas

because from the beginning of Orpí's expedition, Nueva Barcelona was thought of as such. After some years the whole "city" moved to a new site on the opposite bank of the Neverí to find, at last, its definitive and present location.

Throughout Spanish America different materials, customs, economies, geographies, techniques, and cultures concurred to the grid and square — the same scenography for thousands of plays.

One element in the founding of Nueva Barcelona endures today in our vernacular architecture: the willingness of townspeople to perform the rituals that sustain the history and permanence of a town. This process began with that inaugural ceremony, an act of imagination in which, through the feast, adornments, colors, and rituals, the requisites of civilization were imitated.

The campsite near Nueva Barcelona in which the settlers waited is important to our understanding of the town: it is not a place that gives birth to a town, but a concept, an idea.

Not all Spanish-American towns could fulfill an ideal grid. As we have said, a town had to mold to the landscape, to the existing circumstances. In Venezuela some towns originated on virgin land; most, however, merged with existing Indian villages and, in some instances, predominated the original structure. Other villages founded by Spaniards never accomplished the grid and grew somewhat randomly. Today we find different stages in the development of the grid: towns in which a single house stands on each corner of the block, representing an incomplete grid; or the opposite — towns that developed but where decadence reduced them to isolated fragments.

Spanish America is full of sketches of the Escorial, the Roman Castrum, the chess board, Tablada, Santa Fe de Granada, and many other urban plans, including Renaissance versions of an ideal city plan. Such is the platform on which most of our vernacular architecture remembers and reimagines the forms of "the house of the master" inherited from Spain: alongside new propositions, both subtle and aggressive, that continuously present themselves before the vernacular.

Clockwise: Pueblo Nuevo • Mucuquí • Piñango

1. Pablo Vila, *The Feat of Juan Orpí* (Caracas: Universidad Central de Venezuela, 1975).

STREET

When we enter our towns and cities we perceive and experience them from their streets and plazas, which are critical issues in the founding and construction of the town. The plaza, apart from being the center for collective activities, dictates the town's general proportions, since its width and length determine the size of all the village blocks. Besides communicating the town's components, the street helps the houses to align, forming a series of straight, harmonic patterns.

The following anecdote nicely illustrates the importance of the street and plaza. The town of Carache in the Venezuelan Andes grew with the utmost disorder; two centuries after the town's foundation, its streets still were twisted and its houses isolated randomly. The story goes that, toward the end of the eighteenth century, a Spanish general named Cegarra, for a long time disgusted with the town's disorderly appearance, decided that enough was enough and took upon his hands the task of redesigning Carache. He went to the plaza and, standing on a corner, fired his musket through the maze of houses, aiming toward the outskirts of town; then he ordered his Aide-de-Camp: "See where the bullet's hit the ground? Go there and nail in a stake; then bring a cord from the stake into the plaza." He repeated this operation from the remaining three corners of the square. Carache woke the

following morning full of strings that marked the straight streets to be built. Today Carache has one of the most elegant grids in the Venezuelan Andes.

General Cegarra's method was not a standard one, of course; but, then, one cannot remodel an old town without suitable commotion.

Carache needed a thundering theodolyte capable of redesigning a town and at the same time able to celebrate and announce the event to its people. There was also the need for a technique that could be initiated on a given afternoon with a simple recipe — welcome, celebrated, and understood by all.

From General Cegarra's strings neighbors joined their houses with walls made of wood and mud or, as in the Andes, stone. Thus was marked the block's perimeter, within which new houses were built until a continuous fabric was

formed: that of the street, on which windows and doors appeared as the presence of houses, interiors, and intimacy. That is to say, the street was formed by the walls, homogeneous and public; the house, with its odd, personal openings, represented privacy within the collective.

Top: Jajoí
Bottom: La Mesa

Top: Baragua
Bottom: Altagracia
• Capatárida

Top: Capatárida
Bottom: Plaza de
Santiago • Plaza
de Sabana Grande

Top: Quisiro
Bottom: Piedra
Grande

Top: Choroní
Bottom: Agua
Larga

After colonial times the dialogue between continuous white walls and those personally decorated doors and windows became more complex and unpredictable. The Wars of Independence suddenly opened the country to the vast offerings of the nineteenth century. The changes that ensued are well illustrated by a man and an epoch, Antonio Guzmán Blanco, who ruled Venezuela around the last quarter of the nineteenth century. Inspired by Paris, Blanco ordered significant changes made in Caracas that in turn extended to the provincial city. Let us mention some of his interventions.

Blanco implemented a plan of Caracas in which the city grid for the first time was not idealized: the blocks were not of equal size but instead were represented truthfully by their actual measures and irregularities. Along with this plan he ordered a comprehensive census of properties, and thus the blocks drawn within this survey appeared not as one urban unit but as several unequal lots within one perimeter. He also razed many colonial buildings and replaced them with buildings of free facades that generated "dents" and protuberances along the "street-wall," so that the new architecture became independent from the colonial urban structure.

For the celebration of the Simón Bolívar Centennial, Blanco organized a grand urban feast that forever changed the city's appearance: he built promenades and boulevards and replaced eaves with cornices in all the houses; he also required that neighbors repaint their houses with oil-based paint, which allowed for bright colors, instead of the traditional quicklime, which made all walls look the same. People adorned and painted their walls with cornices and colors that differed from those of their neighbors; privacy gained value and extension; the individual exerted dominion over the collective.

And so it was that new colors, materials, forms, conceptions, vocabularies, ruptures, and departures met in the streets and squares, in the doors and windows. Cegarra was not the sole designer of colonial towns, nor was Guzmán Blanco the only one to modify the rules of colonial urbanism. What we have tried to illustrate are two stages, two contexts, two languages: on the one hand, colonial times, towns, and a vocabulary based on restrictions; on the other, the republican period, the city, and a vocabulary based on the illusion of resources.

General Cegarra's shootings and strings and Blanco's cornices and oil paint suggest how the vernacular departed from the colonial and commenced its own search. From Blanco onward, *verna* would reflect the image of infinite masters.

Clockwise: Quisiro • Canoabo • Quisiro

H O U S E

The urban history of the Venezuelan vernacular house is stubborn, and in some ways its obstinancy exceeds its usefulness. Some isolated ranch houses appear as small towns, and some even smaller villages, with their vacuums, proportions, and rigors, await the possibility of becoming cities.

When we were traveling the northeast environs of Lake Maracaibo, while driving through a dusty plain a lonely and freshly painted house suddenly appeared before us. Loneliness and fresh paint make unlikely partners, but there was something stranger still: the little house had a gay, attractive main facade, but its side walls were made of raw, unadorned, and unpainted mud, without windows. It was as if a piece of street had been cut from somewhere and tossed at random into the middle of nothingness. The road on which we found the house links the towns of Puertos de Altagracia and Quisiro, and that little house could have belonged to either of them: had it been larger and painted in stronger colors, to Puertos de Altagracia; if slimmer and lower, to Quisiro. Thus it was caught in the middle of two styles, a piece both urban and rural.

In rows: San Isidro de Ceuta • Tucacas • Quisiro • Los Roques • Maracaibo • Puertos de Altagracia

In rows: Maracaibo • Maracaibo • Puertos de Altagracia • Los Roques • Los Roques • Paraguaná • Quisiro • San Rafael de Mucuchies • Paraguaná

In rows: Los Roques • Los Roques • Quisiro • Los Roques • Los Roques • Agua Larga • Puertos de Altagracia • San Sebastían • Los Roques

In rows: Quisiro •
Gibraltar •
Quisiro •
Capatárida •
Capatárida •
Maracaibo • San
Luis de la Sierra •
Capatárida •
Casigua

I think this house could well be our Venezuelan "Adam's House in Paradise," now a bit lost in time and space.[1] In 1678 the bishop of Vigevano, Caramuel Lobkowitz, imagined the Hispanic Indian chief living, since years prior to the Spanish Conquest, in a classically conceived palace built of mud. But this chief's House in Paradise, if it ever existed at all, was no more; "classical" in Spanish America meant a house within the grid, a house that stemmed from Spain's centralized program for urbanizing America.

We have discussed how some Renaissance urban theories became peremptory needs of Spain's endeavor to populate. For example, some cities were founded officially but for a long period were not more than ten houses large; thus Alberti's phrase "the city is a big house and the house a small city" is in this case a literal description of that which Spain intended. The South-American town did not originate as the gradual summation of dwellings; it was born of an orderly prefiguration. Each house had a plan, a destiny; each had been conceived as a piece of stuffing with which to fill the city.

Pedregal

Top: Jadaquiva
Bottom: Paraguaná

Top: Capatárida
Bottom: Los Robles
• Agua Larga

In rows: Puertos
de Altagracia •
Tucacas • Ortiz •
Chiguará

In rows: Paraguaná
• Paraguaná •
Capatárida •
Paraguaná • Santa
Rita

In rows: Mitare •
Carache •
Paraguaná •
Paraguaná • Piedra
Grande • Mitare •
Paraguaná •
Paraguaná •
Amuay

Top: San Isidro de
Ceuta
Bottom: Sinamaica
• San Isidro de
Ceuta

Sinamaica

What happened when that relationship changed? What became of those houses when the city no longer understood its parts, when the city used other kinds of urbanism? Currently there are many vernacular versions of dwellings that try to conform to new contexts. But our attention turns more eagerly to a house that no one recognizes any longer, a house full of clues to a city that surrounds it no more, that has a patio that resembles no square, corridors that are the intimate continuation of no street, a house that was once the most anonymous and universal part of the city and now waits like a vestigial, incomprehensible, inhabited ruin.

The Venezuelan writer Ben Ami Fihman describes this situation in a narrative piece called "The House," from which I now extract:

You entered the house from within, and you exited from outside. The rooms, each one fitted with a bidet and a woman, like those insects that have their meat inside and the bones outside, were in the periphery. The main facade was visible only from the drawing room. The patio, which we were constantly encountering, was at the center and anywhere, in every part and in none, as if lying about. Its floors resembled a giant tortoise shell. The sun penetrated its cracks. It was night. I ascended to the cellar and descended to the terrace, to watch the sun from the former, the moon from the latter.

The music, coming from somewhere, resembled a cage. Corridors ran across, not along, and sometimes a tilt in the floor made me walk sideways, like a horse. The room windows faced other rooms, and some windows were frescoes in which the neighboring room was pictured, in the bottom of which there was another window revealing the next chamber.[2]

Fihman describes a single house entered by chance while walking through the city. But each image could be a piece of another house, maybe the grand colonial mansion, or the semi-empty small house that seems to await a new opportunity in our villages. Even more suggestive is the title of the book to which "The House" belongs: *The Resources of Limbo.* The title is a clue to understanding the current

vernacular house and the tradition to which it belongs: it is a house that feeds on solitude, urban inertia, memories, and secrets; a house that waits in limbo because of its ancestry.

1. For this term I am indebted to Joseph Rykwert. See Joseph Rykwert, *On Adam's House in Paradise: The Idea of the Primitive Hut in Architectural History* (New York: Museum of Modern Art, 1972).
2. Ben Ami Fihman, *The Resources of Limbo* (Caracas: Monteavila Editores, 1981).

Clockwise: Mitare • Agua Larga • Vía Tinaquillo

Top: San Lorenzo
Bottom: Vía el
Tocuyo

Top: Pueblo
Nuevo de Mérida
• Camino a
Baragua
Bottom: Santa
Isabel

Top: Guarenas
Bottom: Vía
Piñango • Piñango

Top: Lezama •
Agua Larga
Bottom: Vía
Piñango

Top: Valencia •
Paraguaná
Bottom: La Trampa

Top: Baragua •
San José de
Mérida
Bottom: Piedra
Grande • El
Cayude

Top: Vía Canagua
• Jadacaquiva
Bottom: Paraguaná
• Sebastopol
Paraguaná

Top: Agua Larga
Bottom: Agua
Clara

ORNAMENT

The greatest liberty taken by the urban grid in Spanish America was its absence. Such is the case in the town of San Sebastián, on Margarita Island, which seems to challenge all rules and traditions with straight streets running in unpredictable directions. No one ever thought to rearrange San Sebastián; its corners have delightfully bizarre angles that return us unknowingly to our departure point. On the day we walked its streets all the doors to the houses were open, offering a gallery of interiors, a series of

Overleaf: Los
Roques
This page:
Capatárida

intimacies. Thus we noticed that
many of them had a brightly
colored pilaster in the drawing
room, each of a different color but
placed in the same spot from one
drawing room to another.

We inquired about the origin
and reason for the pilasters and
received a simple answer: Some
years before, a house builder
achieved success in view of the
speed and low cost with which he
built; he also knew the
fundamentals of beauty and
proportion. This builder's only
defect was his obsession with
placing a pilaster in the drawing
room of every house he built. His
widely accepted and persevering
habit made us understand
something that recorded here today
may appear irrelevant, but that in
San Sebastián — in its houses,
streets, windows, and door latches
— is obvious and relevant:
*vernacular architecture is not
anonymous.* Everything we were
seeing had an author, a fact known
to the townspeople who, besides,
remembered him and his fantasy.
The anecdote ends here, however,
because in writing this I cannot
remember the builder's name, an

important piece of information for anyone interested in building a house in San Sebastián but unnecessary to these notes, both for writer and reader.

There are two ways to isolate vernacular architecture from history: one is to label it anonymous (because history needs names, there is no way to survive, historically, without them); the other occurs when the work of a "vernacular" architect is so remarkable, so evidently personal, that it becomes "un-anonymous."

In the latter case the vernacular architect is seen as an exception, a misplaced person possessed by imprecise forces, extracted from his environment like a curiosity. Ironically, the vernacular architect understands and exists only in strict relation to his environment.

These extremes we call the anonymous and the genial are a deformed reflex of the personal and the collective, a relationship in which ornament participates constantly. Ornament is not only

the expression of an individual within the collective, but of an epoch within all others. This was a favorable condition for the adventures and misadventures of Venezuelan vernacular architecture after colonial times. Once Spain had created a system of towns in America, each town had before itself urban development's contradiction: to do and undo itself, to grow old and renew itself.

Maracaibo

Top: Maracaibo
Bottom: San Juan
de Las Galdonas

Maracaibo

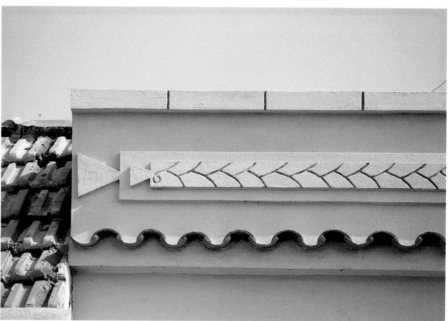

Top: Capatárida •
Maracaibo
Bottom: Maracaibo
• Maracaibo • La
Guardia

Maracaibo

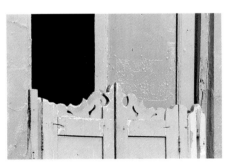

Top: Guayacan •
Torococo
Bottom: Maracaibo

Top: La Mesa •
Guanape • Casigua
Bottom: Barbacoas
• Carache •
Puertos de
Altagracia

Top: Maracaibo •
La Vela de Coro •
Puertos de
Altagracia
Bottom: Quisiro •
Baragua • Rio
Caribe

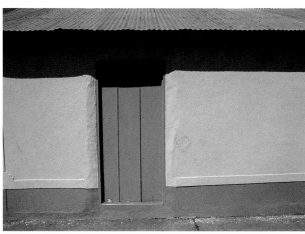

In rows: Camino de Agua Larga • Jadacaquiva • Paraguaná • Guanape • Piedra Grande • Jadacaquiva • Jadacaquiva

In rows: Puertos de Altagracia • Capatárida • Casigua • Puertos de Altagracia

Black, Aboriginal, and Hispanic elements contributed to the building of our towns. This overlay of visions became more complicated still when our vernacular architecture started peeking at the bewildering range of possibilities offered by the nineteenth and twentieth centuries. With insufficient resources, each town became dependent on a medium capable of delivering the illusion of overwhelming diversity. The most widely used device in Venezuelan architecture was ornament, and within it, color.

Color is two-dimensional, flat; it is a lightweight method for creating illusion. Color is also a medium for historical narrative: it can carry references and multiple readings and suggest techniques and styles.

The ancient Greek statue illustrates the history of the relationship between color and form. Some historians have celebrated (while others have discreetly overlooked) the fact that after leaving the sculptor's atelier the statue would receive a coat of paint, makeup, clothes, sandals, earrings, collars, and bracelets.

The statue, today naked, and of which sometimes all that remains is a classical thigh, a hand, or a head, recalls the condition of the Spanish-American city grid: sometimes standing complete, sometimes half-empty and reduced to remains, the border of a square, or the facade of a church — just enough fragments to imagine the whole and its ruling principles. By the same token, the gay cloth and color of the Greek statue resemble the changing and vigorous decoration of our vernacular architecture, whose authors are destined to the same anonymity as those tailors, jewellers, and makeup artists who contributed to the life of the sculpture.

Throughout history towns have dressed and undressed themselves, put on and removed their makeup. There are white towns, clay towns, and towns of bizarre colors. Color adjusts to climate, resource, landscape, and human condition, but its goal remains the same: to be bold and challenging. Since colonial times the pursuit of this goal has been modified by a chromatic instance particularly suited to the region's circumstances. Color has not stopped changing, however; it just happens that there are regions in which this evolution is slow and parsimonious, others in which it is agitated and passionate.

A house is painted year after year with different colors to preserve it physically and symbolically. If a house is not repainted it becomes sad and old; thus, the only way to keep it alive is to continually make it seem different. The more difficult the situation of the house, the livelier, bolder, and more outstanding its colors.

In rows: Dabajuro • El Molino • El Molino • Jadacaquiva • San Francisco de Macaira • Mitare

In rows: Santa Rita
• Tucacas •
Capatárida •
Capatárida •
Tucacas • Pedregal

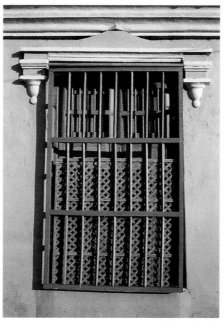

In rows: Aragua de
Barcelona •
Clarines •
Altagracia •
Choroní • Mitare

In rows: Puertos de Altagracia • Capatárida • Capatárida • Quisiro • Baragua • Zaraza • Pueblo Nuevo de Paraguaná

C H U R C H

Toward the end of the
eighteenth century Bishop
Mariano Martí traveled
the province of Venezuela
to examine the general condition of
the land's temples. During this
journey he wrote two diaries: the
official one tells of damaged roofs
and unfinished altars, and contains
a census of people baptized; the
other is his personal diary and
describes the landscape and roads
traveled, gossip on priests, and
stories of the great and minute sins
of the settlers he met.

Overleaf: Agua
Larga
This page:
Tacarigua

The personal diary tells of how, year after year, the town of Mapiare (today called Agua Larga) had no priest among its residents. "Given that it is such an ill-prone place, no one can be found serving Mapiare nor intending to do it, so that about ten years have passed without a priest." The town's church was in poor condition: "Its walls are crumbled, so as to fall to the ground, and its fabric generally lost." Bishop Martí concluded that the best solution was to do away with Mapiare and apportion its residents evenly among neighboring villages. "And regarding its church, it better be torn down once and for all and in such a hot place none be rebuilt, so that those Indians will not return to Mapiare." The residents did not take kindly to his proposition and decided to remain in town, as Martí suspected they would. " … I have received news from San Luis's priest, in a letter dated 30th November 1773, in which he informs me that the Indians of Mapiare do not want to leave their territories, and that they have already rebuilt their run-down church."

Two centuries had passed when we visited Mapiare, and it still lacked a priest. On the day of our visit the townspeople were repairing the church for the upcoming Holy Week festivities. Current restoration included not only new tiles for the roof and floors and new whitewash on the walls, but light bulbs, guitar strings, fresh red paint for the wounds of the Christ image and new thorns for its crown, a replacement finger for a saint's image, mending of the Virgin's dress, and a retouching of Cireneo's lips, on which the hot local climate had implanted an expression of stupor.

From the outside Mapiare's church appears both fragile and eternal, sensuous and unalterable. Through the years its interior has varied with continuous restoration. Today the saint images look like puppets whose wardrobes change each century — like Greek statues not yet undressed.

From left:
Tacarigua •
Torococo • Puerto
Colombia

In rows: San Jose
de Ceutas • Via
Altagracia •
Tuñame • Agua
Larga • Agua
Larga • Goajira

In rows: Quíbor •
Borojó • Los
Roques • Los
Roques • Píritu •
Mitare

The story of the Mapiare church explains that Spain, represented by the figure of Bishop Martí, decided to abandon a village because of its harsh and priest-proof geography. The Spanish priest was some sort of climatological index: that which after three centuries Spain could not master, she declared unlivable. The picture is clear: the vernacular endures even after civilization withdraws. At the same time, the church is the symbol and epicenter for Mapiare's survival and identity.

The other subject for reflection stems not from the church as a historical fact but as an architectural work. Its beauty and interest lie in the abundance of points of view: the vernacular and the classical, the recent interventions and the inherited rites, the doubts and the dogmas, the dedicated work of Mapiare's

people and our sentimental observation; the possibilities are wide and humble. The church has something of essay and remembrance; it still invites Bishop Martí, half repented, half amazed, to return and approve of it finally.

In rows: Pueblo
Nuevo • La Cruz
de Taratara •
Agua Larga •
Rancho de Lazaro
• Agua Larga

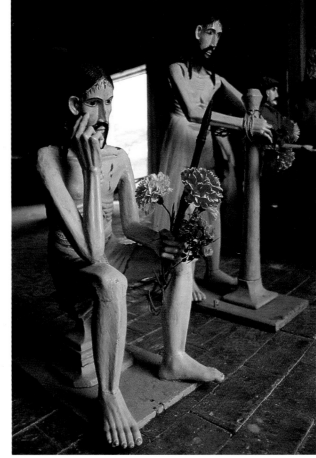

Agua Larga

Top: Santa Isabel
Bottom: El Tupi
Overleaf: Araya

Architecture is remodeled each
time it becomes overwhelmed by
change or boredom, and it finds
extremes that serve as temporary
shelter. Perhaps in these swift
swings from one extreme to
another, from dogma to dogma,
architecture best displays its
infinite spectrum. Those extremes
with more problems to solve and
achievements to enjoy are those we
call popular and learned or
vernacular and civilized. This is
the objective of the images
presented here: to shorten the
distance between these extremes.